MW01298668

THE POWE
HOW GOD CREATED US TO HAVE A CHAMPION SPIRIT

TINA BLACK & BRIANNA BLACK-PETROS

BE

BE UNCOMMON

Trilogy Christian Publishers
A Wholly Owned Subsidiary of Trinity Broadcasting Network
2442 Michelle Drive
Tustin, CA 92780

Copyright © 2020 by Tina Black & Brianna Black-Petros

All Scripture quotations, unless otherwise noted, taken from THE HOLY BIBLE, NEW INTERNATIONAL VERSION®, NIV® Copyright © 1973, 1978, 1984, 2011 by Biblica, Inc.® Used by permission. All rights reserved worldwide.

Scripture quotations marked (KJV) taken from *The Holy Bible, King James Version*. Cambridge Edition: 1769.

All rights reserved, including the right to reproduce this book or portions thereof in any form whatsoever.

For information, address Trilogy Christian Publishing
Rights Department, 2442 Michelle Drive, Tustin, Ca 92780.
Trilogy Christian Publishing/ TBN and colophon are trademarks of Trinity Broadcasting Network.

For information about special discounts for bulk purchases, please contact Trilogy Christian Publishing.

Manufactured in the United States of America

Trilogy Disclaimer: The views and content expressed in this book are those of the author and may not necessarily reflect the views and doctrine of Trilogy Christian Publishing or the Trinity Broadcasting Network.

10 9 8 7 6 5 4 3 2 1

Library of Congress Cataloging-in-Publication Data is available.

ISBN 978-1-64773-048-2 (Print Book)
ISBN 978-1-64773-049-9 (ebook)

FOREWORD

I am so excited for Tina and Brianna's new book. This book challenges us not to be stuck in a common, regular, and normal life. They take us step by step through their wonderful principles that will help us to Be Uncommon in every area of our lives. These two writers are equipped to show us the way.

— Tim Storey

CONTENTS

WHY WE HAD TO WRITE THIS BOOK 7
    Meet Brianna 7
    Meet Tina 9
    You Were Meant To BE UNCOMMON 11

Chapter 1: UNCOMMON PLANS 13
    Find Your Purpose 15
    The Secret Is In The Walking 23
    The Rule Of Five 28
    Step 1 Exercise: Scriptures For Uncommon Plans 32

Chapter 2: UNCOMMON THOUGHTS 35
    Authentic Journaling 41
    Hit The Delete Button 44
    Power Statements 50
    Unlock The Power Of Praise 54
    Step 2 Exercise: Scriptures For Uncommon Thoughts 59

Chapter 3: UNCOMMON FRIENDS 61
    Understand Your Value 63
    Stalk Visionaries And The Power Of Proximity 67
    Who Can You Add To Your Circle? Who Can You Stalk? 69
    Step 3 Exercise: Scriptures For Uncommon Friends 73

Chapter 4: UNCOMMON DISCIPLINE 75
    See Yourself As God Sees You 83
    You're On God's Payroll 87
    You Are Armed And Dangerous 89
    Step 4 Exercise: Scriptures For Uncommon Discipline 94

THE POWER OF LEGACY 97
ACKNOWLEDGMENTS 101
ADDITIONAL RESOURCES 101
ABOUT THE AUTHORS 103

WHY WE HAD TO WRITE THIS BOOK

Before we begin, we'd like to take a moment to introduce ourselves. We are mother and daughter, but most important, we are Christian women who passionately believe in sharing our faith. Whether you are Christian or not, whether you believe in God or have some doubt, we have written this book for *you*. We believe that everyone can and deserves to live an uncommon life, and we believe that the stories, quotes, and shared experiences in this book will start you on your own path to truly BE UNCOMMON.

Meet Brianna

Growing up, I was blessed with a loving family who taught me the foundation for my life: my faith. I've always loved Jesus and had a passion to know Him and experience more of Him. As I grew older, I recognized the gifts and callings God placed in me, including the ability to see people grow and discover the purpose God placed in them. I've always known that leadership would be part of my life, and I believe we are all called to lead and be leaders. There is power in legacy, and I was blessed to be raised in an empowering and leading family. We get to choose what the next generation will experience, based on our ability to be good stewards who use what we've been given.

Part of my journey has always been to see the promises fulfilled in my life and to know what God is speaking in every season. I believe God is always speaking over us and in us, and I'm excited for *you* to have your own personal revelation as we start this journey together. Do not limit what God can do through the lens of your life, but rather watch what God can do through the lens of eternity and your legacy. Your story is powerful. I hope that reading about my mom's and my stories and experiences will inspire you to live the abundant life God has for you. I pray that you will enter into all of heaven's resources as you have greater revelation of your identity as a son or daughter of the King.

In 2011, when I was nineteen years old, I had a "marking moment" with the Lord. During a worship service, I went into an open vision and the Holy Spirit showed me teaching cosmetology skills to a specific group of people. It was like watching a movie. God gave me a vision of myself stomping on injustice and setting captives free. The vision was symbolic and also strategic for planning my next steps. For the next six years, God proved His faithfulness as I chose to step out and partner with His plans for me.

We often have awesome encounters with the Lord—feel-good experiences—but we leave without knowing what to do next. When we learn to fulfill the promises God has spoken over us, we come into the fullness of our identity. The thing that is so cool about God and understanding our purpose is that God actually placed our gifts and desires inside us before we were born, so an encounter in His presence confirms who we already are. God's plans are good! They are meant to prosper us, not harm us. We are so unique in the way God designed us: He wants us to do the things we love to do and the things at which we are naturally gifted because He made us that way. God wants to partner with us to see His will in our lives. Life is meant to be enjoyed: we should live the lives that fulfill us. When we wake up on Monday mornings, we should say, "Thank God it's Monday because I get to live a life I *love!* I have the opportunity to pursue what I naturally love to do." That is the joy of following Jesus and discovering who we were always meant to be.

Meet Tina

When I was sixteen years old, I wrote a suicide note to my family. Two years later, God pulled me out of a pit of depression and despair when my sister told me about having faith in Jesus Christ. It was the first time I'd heard about Jesus dying for me. On that day, I knew I had a purpose and I knew I had a legacy to fulfill. Everything seemed to become crystal clear. I've saved that note all these years to remind myself of God's incredible goodness and that He loves me so much, He died for me.

My sister gave me a manual and a cassette tape (I know, I'm dating myself) by an author whose name I can't recall. The author told the story of a man who worked on a railroad. One day, his son came to work with him and was playing on the tracks. A train was coming from a distance and, in that moment, the man had two choices: to derail the train, letting it crash and kill many of the people on board, or to let the train run over his son and kill him. His son was killed that day to save all the people on that train, and not one of them had any idea what the man had done. That is just like God allowing His son Jesus to die in our place to save all the people, and most of us have no idea what God did for us. Most of us either never hear this or choose not to hear because we don't feel worthy of such a sacrifice.

Years later, when my husband told me, "Tina, I'm going to buy a cosmetology school because I think it will be a ministry for you," it was another marking moment in my life. I was fourteen years into the dentistry business, but as soon as I heard the word *ministry*, I was in. I had felt an empty space in my heart at the time but suddenly saw a vision of turning a business into a ministry.

Six months into owning that school, a student told me she had tried to commit suicide the night before. As I coached and mentored her, I suddenly knew why I had gone through my own challenges and written my own suicide note at age sixteen. I shared my story and told her how I had found true meaning and purpose for my life. A listening ear and caring heart were all she needed. I convinced her to get therapy, and to this day she is doing amazingly well. Since then, I've had the opportunity to mentor and minister to many people. I am so grateful to that student for showing me that I could turn a business into a ministry and helping me realize that our greatest adversities can lead to our greatest assignments.

Each year, I choose a word to live by. In 2016, my word was *uncommon*. I've always known I'm uncommon; I'm definitely not like most people I know. I am extremely driven and can run circles around people half my age. Brianna has always been uncommon, too, and such an inspiration to me. While writing separate speeches for a women's retreat we'd been invited to address, we immediately knew that our topic would be "Be Uncommon: The Power of Legacy and Living a Champion Spirit"…and now it's the title of this book!

You Were Meant To BE UNCOMMON

What does *uncommon* mean to us? The dictionary defines it as "out of the ordinary, unusual, extraordinary, outlandish, unconventional." We're constantly reminded of these scriptures, too:

- "Do not conform to the pattern of this world" (Romans 12:2).
- "Do not love this world nor the things it offers you" (1 John 2:15, NLT).
- "Do not be yoked together with unbelievers" (2 Corinthians 6:14).
- "You are the light of the world. A town built on a hill cannot be hidden" (Matthew 5:14).

We believe that God did not put any of us on earth to live common or average lives. He calls His children to greater destinies. And let us tell you this: if you were born, you *are* a child of God. You're an incredible miracle. Not one person has your specific DNA, your talents, or your purpose to fulfill. You were born to live an uncommon life, and this book will help you do just that!

God has placed gifts, callings, and promises over each one of us. You were called to impact the world and leave a legacy no one else can. Have you seen the popular quote these days: BE YOU? Too many of us are trying to be someone we aren't. This book encourages you to become the extraordinary and uncommon person God has called you to be—not a version of someone you follow on TV or social media.

As Ephesians 2 says,

> We have become His poetry, a re-created people that will fulfill the destiny He has given each of us, for we are joined to Jesus, the Anointed One. Even before we were born, God planned in advance our *destiny* and the good works we would do to *fulfill* it!
> Ephesians 2:10 (TPT)

We know God will use this book for His glory, and we can't wait to share with you some practical principles for living an uncommon life. Are you ready to discover the four steps to being uncommon? Be sure to do the exercises at the end of each step. That's where the real magic lives!

Step 1

UNCOMMON PLANS

Brianna:

The first step to living an uncommon life is to have uncommon plans. This is spoken to us in Habakkuk 2:2 (ESV), which says, "Write the vision; make it plain on tablets, so He may run who reads it."

How do we make an uncommon plan? We start by understanding God's purpose for us. It doesn't help to make a plan unless we first identify our purpose. A bunch of to-do lists without a purpose is just busy work! Knowing who we are, knowing our core values, and having vision determines the course of our lives.

For me, finding my purpose happened when my passion and skill aligned with what God had spoken over me in the encounter I mentioned earlier, when I saw the vision of myself teaching cosmetology skills and setting captives free. When we seek encounters with the Lord, we are actually seeking His heart. If we want to have an encounter with God, we need to spend some time alone with Him and ask Him what His heart holds for us. We need to ask Him, "What did you create me for that would give me the most fulfilment in life?" God loves to speak to His children. He is a good father and does not withhold His goodness from us.

Before we understand our purpose, we must take a journey with the Lord. This is not a self-discovery book. Before we "find" ourselves or discover how or why we were created, we must go to the creator Himself. The more we understand our creator, the more we will find ourselves there. If we want to understand how a car is made, we don't go to our banker. Although he might be able to give us some wisdom or share some of his experiences about cars, we won't find the exact details of how a car is made until we go directly to the one who made the car. The same goes with God and discovering how He created us. Each of us is unique to Him and only He can tell us our purpose.

Many people go through their entire lives without truly knowing themselves or their purpose. They let the world tell them who they are, or they define themselves by their experiences, failures, successes, and hurts. But *only* God can tell us who we are and why He created us. God's biggest desire has always been relationship: He wants to do life *with* us. We might have a good idea on our own, but is it a God idea? God, who created us, who gives us breath in our lungs and loves us unconditionally, delights in speaking a "now word" or a "spoken word" in this present moment. The Greek word for this is *rhema*, which literally means "utterance" or the instant, personal speaking of God to us. God also speaks to us through the Bible, which is the inspired living Word of God; the Greek word for that is *logos*. Yes, God still speaks today.

I've been a follower of Jesus my entire life and *every* time I pick up the Bible, I get fresh revelation. I could read the same verse a thousand times and still get something new from it. That's because God's Word is living. Hearing God comes in multiple forms, because He is a multifaceted God. Hearing God's voice starts with surrender: surrendering our whole lives and hearts to Him. In Matthew 16:24 (ESV), Jesus says, "If anyone would come after me, let Him deny himself and take up His cross and follow me." It starts with our *yes*.

FIND YOUR PURPOSE

Brianna:

When we apply what Jesus has already paid for and realize that we work *from* victory, not *for* victory, then just like that, we'll work *from* our purpose, not *for* our purpose. When we understand that we already have these things inside us, we can begin to tap into what the Lord has already spoken over us.

All God's promises are yes and amen. This means when we align ourselves with Him, when we go after our purpose in life and take it by force, He confirms us and agrees with us. There's a grace and a favor released in our lives when we wholeheartedly and relentlessly pursue our God-given purpose and destiny. When we go into the presence of God, we pull down the realities of heaven, and that reality becomes our reality.

Before my parents owned their cosmetology school, my dad used to take me there to get my hair done. I was six years old and I would say, "Daddy, will you buy this school for me?" What kind of six-year-old asks their dad, "Will you buy this business for me?"

I believe God was speaking prophetically and birthing a legacy and vision through six-year-old me. No matter your age or your qualifications, God will use you. It's so amazing that God speaks promises for us before we are even born. We just have to tap into the natural passions and skillsets inside us and partner with the Holy Spirit to see those promises come to pass. God loves to call the unqualified! In Matthew 18:2, Jesus says we must become like little children to enter the kingdom of God. That's because little children have no fear of what people think; they believe that anything is possible and they can do whatever they desire in life. As we get older, we start putting limitations on ourselves, getting in the way of our own dreams.

"Don't let anyone look down on you because you are young, but set an example for the believers in speech, in conduct, in love, in faith, and in purity" (1 Timothy 4:12).

I was raised in a home that never lacked and always believed in God for the impossible. That's why as a naïve six-year-old girl, I asked for something I did not have: because I saw it, I had desire for it, God breathed His breath on it, and it came to pass. Seven businesses later and we still believe in God for more.

I've heard it said, "What is the difference to God between $500 and $5 million? Nothing!" It's all in our perspective and our faith capacity to believe. What are you asking God to provide? Is your faith based on your limitations and resources, or is it based on God's unlimited resources? Dream bigger! No matter how young or old you are, God can use you.

Tina:

It's not wrong to have a plan, but always ask God to confirm your plan, and if He has something else in mind, be willing to give it over to Him. If you're too consumed or locked into *your* plan, you'll miss God's prompting and gentle leading by the Holy Spirit. Constantly be in the "flow" of His spirit. Always pray first and ask for His plan, and the Holy Spirit will guide and direct you. There is freedom in His plan that gives us joy, no matter what He chooses for us. As it says in 2 Corinthians 3:17, "Now the Lord is the Spirit, and where the Spirit of the Lord is, there is freedom."

For years, I was locked into the idea that my life's plan would lie in dentistry, but when my husband told me in 1998 that he felt the beauty industry would be my ministry, I felt God's gentle nudging on my heart. In 2001 when I met Winn Claybaugh and John Paul DeJoria, owners of Paul Mitchell Schools, I could feel God's prompting of the Holy Spirit that the Paul Mitchell company would help me take my ministry to another level. Years later, in 2013 I found myself becoming a John Maxwell coach and training under John C. Maxwell himself. As he prayed the Holy Spirit into the room, tears ran down my face as I received the gift of speaking in tongues and knew I was in the room that would forever change my life. That day, the Holy Spirit transformed me into the person God designed me to be, and I have never been the same. I have felt so much freedom and joy.

Something God repeatedly spoke to me in 2017 was Ephesians 3:20, God "is able to do immeasurably more than all we ask or imagine, according to His power that is at work in us." I claim that over you right now. It has changed my life and it can change yours, too.

I want to encourage you to dream big.

- "'For my thoughts are not your thoughts, neither are your ways my ways,' declares the Lord. 'As the heavens are higher than the earth, so are my ways higher than your ways and my thoughts than your thoughts'" (Isaiah 55:8–9).
- "Nothing they have imagined they can do will be impossible for them" (Genesis 11:6, AMP).
- In the book *Switch On Your Brain* (chapter 12), Dr. Caroline Leaf states that "imagination, visualization, deep thought and reflection produce the same physical changes in the brain as would physically carrying out the same imagined processes."

UNCOMMON PLANS

One of the ways I dream big is to make a vision or dream board every year. One of my favorite ways includes good old-fashioned poster board and glue. For three months before the end of each year I collect magazines, words, and pictures. I love Pinterest, too—I "pin" anything that looks interesting to me. Right before the end of the year, I reflect on what matters to me and write my dream for the next year. I put it on my poster board, hang it on my office wall, take a picture of it, and make it my computer wallpaper. I even make a copy to carry in my briefcase so it's always with me as I travel. I look at my vision board and pray over it throughout the year. I also have all of my team members, leadership workshop attendees, and online mastermind listeners do this activity and they love it. We have a "reading" of the dream boards that I learned from one of my coaches years ago, and they enjoy that, too. It's probably everyone's favorite activity because it's a lot of fun, but I also believe it's because God puts dreams deep in our hearts that only He can manifest, and this little bit of creativity really draws them out. It's so beautiful to see the smiles on their faces and the passion that flows from their mouths when my team and workshop attendees experience this.

I encourage you to make a dream board.
Even if it's midyear and you haven't made one before, stop right now and make one.

God does not create us to have an average life.
He calls us to greatness and to step into our destiny and legacy so we can change generations.
God will always make a way when it seems like

there is no way. He will bring dreams to pass
that could never work in the natural world.

I am a first-generation Christian in my home, and I
am changing generations. I've heard it said that one
change in your life can change up to four generations.
One action can affect generations we will never meet.

My husband has an incredible family history book that
one of his cousins put together years ago. John Black
(Bryan's great-great-great-grandfather) was a poor
weaver who was nearly beheaded for crossing cultural
lines and impregnating Janet Campbell, a woman from
a very wealthy family. Janet's cousin was the Duke of
Argyll in Scotland, and back then, poor people never
married wealthy people. Fortunately, Janet pleaded for
John's life; they were married and had five additional
children. Just think: the majority of my husband's
family might have never been born if John had been
beheaded. Talk about changing generations! This story
can be yours: God will make a way when it seems there
is no way. He will open doors that no man can shut.

Last year, while making my dream board, I saw the
word *Hawaii* in a magazine, cut it out, and put it on the
board. I asked myself, *Why am I putting that word on my
board? But okay, I'll just do it.* It was the only vacation
I put on the board: I'm not much of a vacationer
because I really love what I do and I love to work.

At the beginning of the year, I saw an opportunity
on Facebook to donate money to Eyes on Cancer,
which educates people in the beauty industry to

detect possible skin cancer on their clients. Those who donated could enter someone's name to win a trip to the Paul Mitchell Hawaii Hair Show. Our salon was not doing well financially at the time, so I called Shaun, my operations leader, to see if we could donate.

With an amount of money already in mind, I asked, "How much money is in the bank account?"

Shaun said, "A little over $1,000." The exact amount I wanted to give!

"Give it all to Eyes on Cancer under Brianna's name," I said. Two weeks later, guess who won the trip to Hawaii? Brianna! And we went as an entire family.

The doors opened for us because God can do immeasurably more than we can ever ask or imagine. As 1 Corinthians 1:26–29 (TPT) says:

> Brothers and sisters, consider who you were when God called you to salvation. Not many of you were wise scholars by human standards, nor were many of you in positions of power. Not many of you were considered the elite when you answered God's call. But God chose those whom the world considers foolish to shame those who think they are wise, and God chose the puny and powerless to shame the high and mighty. He chose the lowly, the laughable in

> the world's eyes—nobodies—so that
> He would shame the somebodies.
> For He chose what is regarded as
> insignificant in order to supersede
> what is regarded as prominent, so
> that there would be no place for
> prideful boasting in God's presence.

That trip to Hawaii birthed opportunities in my life that only God could open. I spoke at events I never dreamed of addressing, and that catapulted a new coaching and consulting business for salon owners. None of it would have been possible without God's power in my life.

Another dream board item that came true was getting the opportunity to become a speaker in the first place. Years ago, our business partner Winn Claybaugh told all of the Paul Mitchell School owners that we needed to become motivational speakers in our schools. He said we would earn more influence and respect from our teams as well as our students. I literally wanted to crawl under the table when he said that, thinking: *Nope! I am not going to be a speaker. I will never stand up and speak in front of people.* (I must be related to Moses!) For me to stand up in front of audiences today is a God-miracle in my life. It is definitely a gift that only God could have given me, because now it's hard to get me off the stage.

On one of my dream boards, I wrote that I would have speaking engagements with my daughter. At the time, I thought, *I might, I might not,* but guess what? It happened! Many churches and businesses have booked us to speak since I put that on my dream board, and that's what inspired us to write this book together.

How do you know your purpose? First I want to ask you:

- What are you passionate about?
- What are your strengths?

Then I want to encourage you to step right into your passion. Get around the right people, the right cheerleaders, and you will find your purpose. The right people are right in front of you. Take advantage of opportunities you are being given right now. Spend time with people who are living their purpose, ask them to mentor you, ask them questions, and look for opportunities to serve them.

I'm praying today for a breakthrough for you, that you will find your purpose and walk into it. As I heard John C. Maxwell say a few years ago, "The secret is in the walking."

THE SECRET IS IN THE WALKING

Brianna:

My strategy for life has always been to know what God is doing in every season. I challenge you to get alone with God, get in the secret place, and in every season begin to ask God: "What are you doing in my family? What are you doing in my career? What are you doing in my relationships?"

God is always speaking. When we are in relationship with Him, just as a loving father and friend would, He speaks to us. He is not a distant God, but a close and intimate God who desires to have a relationship with us.

How can we be certain God is speaking to us and it's not just our own thoughts? In 1 Corinthians 2:16, the Apostle Paul says that all believers "have the mind of Christ," meaning that they share His "plan, purpose, and perspective" (Got Questions Ministries).

Try this exercise: Write down the first thing that comes to your mind. Remember: you have the mind of Christ. From there you can use your discernment to pull out anything that might not be from Him. I promise, you will get so much revelation when you practice hearing God's voice. Keep pursuing Him, surrender your heart and mind to Him, and He will fill you with His thoughts.

Hearing God starts with the understanding and belief that God is always good, He's always in a good mood, and His thoughts for us are good. John 10:10 reminds us that "the thief comes only to steal and kill and destroy; I have come that they may have life, and have it to the full." That is God's desire for us: that we will have life *to the full!*

God is always speaking over us; He does not withhold any good gifts from His children. He wants us to come into the fullness of who we are as His sons and daughters. We are His royal priesthood. He wants us to know who we are, why we were created, and what our destiny and legacy on this earth are. We were meant to rule and reign on earth. We have access to the impossible.

UNCOMMON PLANS

One of the coolest things about being in relationship with God is that He gives us secrets to reigning in life. He gives us God-ideas and strategies to pursue the things we are called to do more effectively.

The Holy Spirit is attracted to movement. When we begin to pursue our purpose and our gifts, the Holy Spirit will partner with us. The Holy Spirit is attracted to movement. The secret is in the walking. It's in the movement and the risk-taking: the scary, unsure, fear-filled moments when we don't know the outcome. But we choose in those moments to trust Him. We have to be comfortable with the uncomfortable. When Peter saw Jesus walking on the water, it was a scary moment: there was chaos all around. But when Jesus called to Peter and said, "Come," Peter walked on the water toward Jesus.

Today, Jesus is saying to us: *Come. Step out of your boat, step out of your comfort zone, and trust me. Don't be concerned by the storms around you.* He wants us to trust Him.

If we want to live a life of miracles in all aspects of our lives, we have to get used to living a life of risk. As it says in 2 Chronicles 16:9, the eyes of the Lord wander the earth, looking for those to land on, and He chooses to land on those of us who begin to take risks and step into our destinies. Sometimes, all it takes is to step forward into our purpose and desires. One step forward. Just an inch. All God needs is our yes. When He tells us our purpose and our destiny, our response must be yes. Humility looks like surrender and our yes looks like trust.

God is asking us today, "Will you humble yourself and surrender your life to me? Will you trust me with your life?" If our answer is yes, we can get ready for the life God designed for us, a life filled with fulfilment, joy, and peace. In every season we will know that because we said yes to God's plan, even our most trying times will be filled with peace.

Tina:

Yes, the secret is in the walking. We'll be a little shaky at first, but that's okay. Keep walking! In my first attempts at "public speaking" to my team and then my students, I failed more times than I want to admit, including one moment in a Paul Mitchell School when I really flopped. But I know it was meant to be part of my story so I could eventually encourage you.

I remember a distinct moment on stage when a student verbally attacked me about what I was saying. As irritated as I felt, I later realized he was right: I needed to get better at my message. Keep practicing, keep speaking, and don't stop. I still mess up from time to time, but when I do, I know it means I need to perfect my message. I need to keep practicing in front of the mirror and videotaping myself to see what I need to work on so when I speak, my message has meaning and impact, adds value to the audience, and encourages them to impact the world the way I've been blessed to do.

Years ago, I lost almost $100,000 when my first salon failed. I was so underqualified to open it: I'm a terrible hairstylist (I can barely comb my own hair) and I was a subpar business owner. When the salon failed, I thought that door was shut, but God had other plans for me. With the right partnerships and the right team, God could supernaturally turn me into the business owner He destined me to be. When we had the opportunity to partner with Ken Paves, a celebrity hairstylist, and our daughter Brianna, in a new salon in 2014, I knew we had to do it not only for my daughter but for myself: to prove that God can use the weak for His purpose. I'm living proof that you don't have to "qualify" to do big things. Opening that salon was such a testimony of "keep walking."

My family has now been given the opportunity to open salons all over the country. God birthed a salon and leadership culture in me that only He could produce and now I am unstoppable. I still struggle with my next move, but I know God will lead, guide, and direct because it's all in His hands this time. When I opened my first salon, I tried to manipulate and control every move, but this time it's different. I feel God's gentle nudging, and the wisdom He has given me to direct and lead the salons is so much better now. Do I make mistakes? Yep. Daily. But I know with God's help and the right people in our business, anything is possible.

I want to encourage you because I've lived a fear-filled life with so much hesitation, but God spoke to me and said, "Fear and hesitation are not from me. You walk in courage because you are mine. You continue to walk." Now it's my turn to tell you: just keep walking. Fail fast. Fail big. And jump right back in again. There's no way I would be where I am today if I didn't embrace failure and keep jumping into it. One of my mantras is, "Failure is my friend." It gives me courage to keep on walking.

THE RULE OF FIVE

Tina:

I've been blessed to be part of the John Maxwell team since 2013. One of the many things I've learned from John is his "rule of five," which says that when we set a goal, we should list the five things we must do daily to bring that goal to fruition. For example, in his goal of being an author, John Maxwell's rule of five looks like this:

1. He reads
2. He files things
3. He thinks
4. He asks questions
5. He writes

Here's my rule of five:

1. **Worship**: I'm part of the 5:00 a.m. club, a fun way of saying that I generally wake up two to three hours before I leave the house. I spend the first twenty minutes in worship, writing in my gratitude journal, and studying my Bible.
2. **Plan:** I spend the next twenty minutes planning my day, week, and month.
3. **Execute:** I identify the top three things I need to complete that day and start on them

immediately. I call this "eat frogs first," meaning I start with the tasks I least want to do that day.
4. **Inspect:** I constantly inspect key areas of my businesses to see what is working, what is not working, and how I can support my team.
5. **Create Magic!** In our Paul Mitchell Schools, "Create Magic!" is one of our culture pieces—fun verbiage for random acts of kindness. I love to create magic for people and give unexpectedly, and I daily look for ways that I can honor and add value to them. Some of my favorite ways are love notes, encouraging texts, random Starbucks treats, gift cards, and hugs. I'm always looking for new ways to create magic for strangers, family, and my team. One of the most recent books I've been studying is Gary Chapman's book: *The 5 Languages of Love in the Workplace*. I'm learning how to appreciate my team in "their" language, not my language. It's been very eye-opening for me!

I encourage you to find your rule of five. As you think of your purpose and look at your dream board, what daily habits do you need to form? What's your rule of five? Define it here:

1.
2.
3.
4.
5.

I consistently pray for wisdom and discernment. Recently, when God exposed a treasure that had always been there, I knew He was speaking right to me. Years ago, one of my kids gave me a plaque with my favorite scripture verse, "For I know the plans I have for you," declares the Lord, "plans to prosper you and not to harm you, plans to give you hope and a future" (Jeremiah 29:11).

That plaque has been sitting on my bathroom counter for years, but that day I felt as if I saw it for the first time. You see, it didn't end at verse 11; the plaque cited three more verses I'd never noticed before. How often do we do quote a verse that's convenient for us at the time, but don't notice the verses around it—the full story?

- Verse 12 says: "Then you will call on me and come and pray to me, and I will listen to you."
- Verse 13 adds: "You will seek me and find me when you seek me with all your heart."
- Verse 14 concludes with: "'I will be found by you,' declares the Lord, 'and will bring you back from captivity. I will gather you from all the nations and places where I have banished you,' declares the Lord, 'and will bring you back to the place from which I carried you into exile.'"

Those verses on the plaque were followed by Psalm 32:8. The maker of this plaque must have known that someone was going to notice this and everything would change:

"I will instruct you and teach you in the way you should go; I will counsel you with my loving eye on you" (Psalm 32:8).

Seriously, drop the mic, that's it! We can't just stop at Jeremiah 29:11! How often do we go our own way without taking time to pray and seek God with all our heart so He can find us and pull us away from being prisoners of this world's values and our own toxic thoughts?

God instructs and teaches us the way we should go by giving us wisdom and discernment and keeping His loving eye on us. How does He do that? Through His Word and prayer—but we have to be diligent and consistent in reading, meditating, and speaking to Him so we can hear His voice. Most of my life, I've been going through the motions. It's easy to get too busy to read His Word, meditate on His Word, and tell ourselves the lie that it's too hard to memorize scripture. That plaque was a game changer for me and I hope it is for you, too!

Now that you know the blueprint for life—now that you know that truly uncommon people have uncommon plans—you will do something *so big* that everyone who knows you will say, "Wow! Only God could have done that!"

STEP 1 EXERCISE: SCRIPTURES FOR UNCOMMON PLANS

Check out these verses that support the fact that, because you are God's child, you are uncommon and God has uncommon plans for you. As you reflect on these verses, write a note below each one about how it applies to you.

- **Habakkuk 2:2**: "Write down the revelation and make it plain on tablets so that a herald may run with it."

- **Ephesians 3:20**: "Now to Him who is able to do immeasurably more than all we ask or imagine, according to His power that is at work within us."

- **Galatians 4:28**: "Now you, brothers and sisters, like Isaac, are children of promise."

- **Ephesians 2:10**: "For we are God's handiwork, created in Christ Jesus to do good works, which God prepared in advance for us to do."

- **1 Corinthians 1:26–27**: "Brothers and sisters, think of what you were when you were called. Not many of you were wise by human standards; not many were influential; not many were of noble birth. But God chose the foolish things of the world to shame the wise; God chose the weak things of the world to shame the strong."

- **Romans 12:6**: "We have different gifts, according to the grace given to each of us. If your gift is prophesying, then prophesy in accordance with your faith; if it is serving, then serve; if it is teaching, then teach; if it is to encourage, then give encouragement; if it is giving, then give generously; if it is to lead, do it diligently; if it is to show mercy, do it cheerfully."

- **Hebrews 13:21 (AMP)**: "Equip you with every good thing to carry out His will and strengthen you (making you complete and perfect as you ought to be) accomplishing in us that which is pleasing in His sight, through Jesus Christ, to whom be the glory forever and ever. Amen."

What verses can you find to add to this list?

Step 2

UNCOMMON THOUGHTS

Brianna:

The most important way to be uncommon and live out God's uncommon plans for us is to have uncommon thoughts.

> Christ's resurrection is your resurrection too. This is why we are to yearn for all that is above, for that's where Christ sits enthroned at the place of all power, honor, and authority! Yes, feast on all the treasures of the heavenly realm and fill your thoughts with heavenly realities, and not with the distractions of the natural realm.
> Colossians 3:1–2 (TPT)

If we've been seated with Christ, then we're seated at the right hand of the Father—literally seated with Jesus—and we need to start envisioning ourselves there.

In that vision comes the right perspective and right thinking, which leads to right believing. We begin to see our challenges not from an earthly perspective but from God's perspective. In those moments of uncertainty or struggle, we can renew our minds and choose peace, joy, love, and hope. God gave us free will so we can choose to think the way He thinks and to have a perspective that is different from the world's perspective.

When we live life fully connected to the Father, we are filled with hope-filled thoughts because God's perspective never shifts. He sees every situation we face and He is with us in those struggles and trials, walking next to us, and He still has hope. Why? Perspective. His thoughts are higher.

God has the ability to have emotion: when we have grief and sadness, He feels it for us, but He always has hope. He sees us going through that breakup and knows that the husband or wife He has chosen is coming soon. He sees us going through that job loss and knows that the job in which we will flourish and succeed is right around the corner. He knows our past, present, and future.

God left His throne and came down as man. He faced every temptation and pain we experience on earth, so He can sympathize with our life experiences. He is fully God yet became fully man on our behalf. He conquered sin, death, and the grave on our behalf. He sees every hurt, pain, season, and high and low we go through. But the best part? He sees us on the other side of that season. A few years ago, our business gave us the opportunity to put this truth to the test.

In 2015, we had a salon walkout. Our entire team, except for one person, went to work somewhere else. This is devastating to any business and it would have been easy for me to toss in the towel, but I knew God's perspective in that moment: He was doing a new thing. He had called me to the salon in the first place and I knew He would see me through it. I saw that challenge from a different perspective, a different vision, and I had hope.

All it takes sometimes is to ask the Lord, "God, give me a new vision. Give me a new perspective because I want to see what you see, Lord." All it takes is the right perspective. One thing I love about Christians and the church is that we are overcomers. God calls us to be overcomers. Revelations 12:11 (KJV) is a good example of this: "And they overcame Him by the blood of the Lamb." If Jesus has overcome, then that makes us overcomers. So wherever He is seated, that's where we're seated, too. That's how we need to view our lives and renew our thoughts.

One of my favorite songs, "God, I Look to You" (Bethel Music Publishing), says:

> God, I look to you, I won't
> be overwhelmed—
> Give me vision to see
> things like you do.
> God, I look to you, you're where
> my help comes from—
> Give me wisdom, you
> know just what to do.

The next time you're facing negative thoughts or a rough season of life, remember this promise from Proverbs 3:5–6: "Trust in the Lord with all your heart and lean not on your own understanding; in all your ways submit to Him, and He will make your paths straight."

Tina:

Brianna is so right: we are overcomers!

- 1 John 5:4 (ESV) says, "For everyone who has been born of God overcomes the world. And this is the victory that has overcome the world—our faith."
- John 16:33 (ESV) says, "I have said these things to you, that in me you may have peace. In the world you will have tribulation. But take heart; I have overcome the world."

Hearing these two verses just gives me so much peace.

When I was in Guatemala with the John Maxwell team teaching leadership, I shared some of my trials with my mentor and coach, Scott Faye. He said something so profound, as if God was speaking through him in my language. He said, "Tina, there is nothing to worry about ever." In that moment, time stopped, and a feeling of peace rushed over me in that instant.

Nothing to worry about. Ever. Just let that sink in.

That became one of my first mantras. When I came home, I taught it to my directors and still teach it to anyone I meet who feels anxious (and that happens all the time). When I share those words, I can feel the tension leave them.

We must learn to control our anxiety and our fear, and the solution is our words. Our words have so much power. Our words help to control our thoughts.

In my success classes, I've always taught this saying (author unknown):

> Be careful of your thoughts, for your thoughts become your words.
>
> Be careful of your words, for your words become your actions.
>
> Be careful of your actions, for your actions become your habits.
>
> Be careful of your habits, for your habits become your character.
>
> Be careful of your character, for your character becomes your destiny.

Proverbs 4:23 (NCV) offers something similar: "Be careful what you think, because your thoughts run your life."

And Philippians 4:8 (NLT) says, "Fix your thoughts on what is true, and honorable, and right, and pure, and lovely, and admirable. Think about things that are excellent and worthy of praise."

I decided a long time ago to talk about my blessings more than my disappointments. This past year, we've had several challenges in our companies. Here's the list, and I'm sure I'm missing a lot more:

1. One of our staff members died suddenly and tragically.
2. Hurricane Irma, one of the worst that Florida has ever seen, hit our home and school and closed our business for a few weeks, causing our company to lose over $60,000.
3. A fire broke out on the roof of our Michigan school, requiring us to completely restore the school and displace our students and clients for five to six weeks at a loss of hundreds of thousands of dollars.

Looking at me, most people would not be able to tell what a rough year it's been, because of my positive attitude. In fact, I'm so positive that I have to think really hard about the bad things that happened because I only see the blessings. My glass is always half full, never half empty, as they say.

No thought entering our minds should ever go unchecked. As Psalm 139:23–24 says: "Search me, God, and know my heart; test me and know my anxious thoughts. See if there is any offensive way in me, and lead me in the way everlasting."

One of the greatest ways to combat negative thoughts is authentic journaling.

AUTHENTIC JOURNALING

Unlike my children, I didn't grow up going to church. As I mentioned at the beginning of this book, I found out about Jesus dying for me when I was eighteen years old. But when I was about twelve years old, I remember grocery shopping with my mom, and seeing a Bible (yes, in a grocery store). I asked my mom to buy it for me, and I remember reading bits and pieces of it often before going to bed. God started working on me when I was twelve years old: I didn't need to be at church to hear what He was telling me. God was speaking directly to me.

> For the word of God is alive and active. Sharper than any double-edged sword, it penetrates even to dividing soul and spirit, joints and marrow; it judges the thoughts and attitudes of the heart.
> Hebrews 4:12

Alive and active...sharper than a double-edged sword. Wow! Let that sink in. When we open God's Word, we cannot escape His love.

The Bible repeatedly refers to God's Word as a "double-edged sword." Ephesians 6:17 calls it the "sword of the Spirit." When we're struggling or frustrated and a message suddenly comes into our minds and sharply cuts right to the chase, it's God's Word dropping into our spirits, cutting through our questions, intellect, and natural logic, and getting deep into our hearts.

Boom! We can't contain it any longer. God's Word inside of us.

Transformation! When we come into agreement with God's Word, He releases a mighty power into our situation.

All the great men and women of God have a God-habit: they know the vital importance of spending time alone with God. Luke 22:39 shows that Jesus had a habit of going to the Mount of Olives to pray. Genesis 5:24 says that Enoch habitually walked with God.

In her book *Switch On Your Brain* (chapter 5), Dr. Caroline Leaf says,

> When we pray, when we catch our thoughts, when we memorize and quote scripture, we move into this deep meditative state. This great state of mind is also activated when we intellectualize deeply about information… We are highly intellectual beings created to have relationship with a highly intellectual God. We should never underestimate how brilliant we are and that we are only limited by how we see ourselves.

Seeking and spending time with God is our most vital need. Authentic journaling is one way I do this.

Have you ever journaled? I don't know who taught me or why it stuck, but I took to journaling as a young lady and I've journaled ever since. I still have those journals today and occasionally I look through them and giggle to myself at all the things I wrote then. (I was obsessed with food and boys...rolling my eyes!) Later in life, I learned how to do "authentic journaling" from Paul Martinelli, president of the John Maxwell team. This tool transformed my life and made me into the author I am today.

Rarely a day goes by when I don't journal. It's like going out of the house without any clothes on; it just isn't happening! I feel lost when I don't spend time journaling.

So, how do you become an authentic journaler? I've tweaked the process and teach it often in my online coaching classes and mastermind groups. Here it is briefly, but you can tweak it to your liking.

1. I wake up and get my coffee.
2. I grab my journal, play some nice soft music, and light a candle.
3. I write the word *Thanks* and start writing what I am grateful for from the previous day.
4. Next I write the word *Prayers* and cry out to God with all my challenges, all my gratitude prayers, and turn it all over to Him.
5. Next is my Bible study. I'm currently doing a devotion with a few books from Christian author and speaker Joyce Meyer, so I usually write what God is teaching me and what action I want to take that day or that week from His Word.

6. Last, I write *Power Thoughts,* another devotion by Joyce Meyer (and a free app you can download), where she literally turns scripture into a power thought. I write what God is speaking to me and meditate on it for a few moments.

My authentic journaling might take ten minutes or sometimes I look up and it's been an hour and a half (some days I get immersed in it). I travel a lot, so I often have to find quiet places in hotels, but my favorite place to journal is in my home office. I love it there. I lock the door so I know no one is watching, and some days I just lie down prostrate and meditate on what God is teaching me. Those are my *best* days.

HIT THE DELETE BUTTON

Tina:
Some days I get off track and compare myself with others, begin to have limiting beliefs, or get frustrated with people at work or in a grocery line. On those days, I have to hit the delete button.

There was a time when I didn't have a right thought process. I mentioned earlier that my first salon had failed. Around 2003, we had a walkout: every team member quit except one person. I'll never forget that day. Some of my team members called me in and calmly told me they were all going to work in other salons. First, I sat there in disbelief. Then I had a panic attack and started crying hysterically. I put my head between my knees because I couldn't breathe and then I ran to the back room and my husband followed.

Bryan told me I needed to pull myself together. He remained calm, as he always does, but I kept telling myself over and over, "You're a failure. You're a failure." Then something snapped inside me and I stopped saying those cruel words to myself. I truly believe the Holy Spirit intervened right then. I wiped my tears, walked back to my team, told them I understood, and wished them all the best. Only one staff member stayed. To this day, I can't begin to tell you how having one person believe in me at that moment affected my life.

Nonetheless, for ten years I was frustrated with that situation. I held in those emotions all those years, blaming everything and everyone around me—the economy, the town, my staff, the industry—everything but myself. In 2013, I had a breakthrough. I was in Guatemala, training the locals on leadership, but actually I was training myself. The course was called "Transformation Begins in Me," and that week I realized that the walkout hadn't happened because the team decided to be jerks that day; it happened because I was a horrible leader. I just didn't see it then; I was blind to it. That week in Guatemala, I not only forgave myself and that entire team, but I also asked for forgiveness from the leaders of my three businesses and promised to become the leader they deserved.

I hit the delete button that day. I forgave my team—and especially myself—and my life was transformed. God started to transform me in ways only He can understand.

In 2 Peter 1:4, the Bible talks about how we can escape the world's corruption caused by human desires. The devil tells us we can't be like God: we can't be merciful and gracious, we can't have joy, we can't be slow to anger and quick to forgive. But the Bible says God has shared His divine nature with us and we can develop it and it can come out of us. We need to stop listening to the devil's lies and hit the delete button. We need to fill our thoughts and words with God's promises.

After that walkout, owning salons was one of those secret dreams I hid in my closet. I was so ashamed of my poor ability to run my salon. I never verbalized my shame or my passion but God knew! In 2014, we got a call from Ken Paves, a celebrity hairstylist and Michigan salon owner. His father was very ill and Ken needed someone to take over his salon. My first thought was, *Oh, I'm a failure. I can't do it.* But then I remembered I had Brianna and I hit the delete button. Brianna could help me run the salon and we would be great together. Several years later, after literally turning the salon around, we accepted a new opportunity to open a chain of salons. It's only the beginning, and I know God has great things in store for our family.

In 2011 at our grand opening in Fort Myers, as I stood on stage with my husband, Brianna, and our son Justin, I remember God saying to me, "One day you'll be on stage with your entire family, telling everyone about me and what I did." And that is starting to come into fruition! I have been given opportunities to speak with each one of them, and my dream is coming to pass. I am overwhelmed with God's kindness. He is turning my failures around. It makes me think of Jeremiah 8:4, which states: "Say to them, 'This is what the Lord says: When people fall down, do they not get up? When someone turns away, do they not return?'" It also makes me think of some verses in Psalm 40:

> He drew me up from the pit of destruction, out of the miry bog, and set my feet upon a rock, making my steps secure. He put a new song in my mouth, a song of praise to our God. Many will see and fear, and put their trust in the Lord.
>
> Psalm 40:2–3 (ESV)

God spoke to me. He said, "Uncommon people have uncommon thoughts, Tina." This hit me so hard as I remembered Romans 12:2: "Do not conform to the pattern of this world." And what is the pattern? It's negativity. Negative thoughts. Anxiety. Depression. An alarming increase in the rate of suicide, up 33 percent from 1999 through 2017 (American Psychological Association, March 2019, Vol. 50, No. 3).

In *Switch On Your Brain* (chapter 4), Dr. Caroline Leaf says,

> The importance of capturing those thoughts cannot be underestimated because research shows that the vast majority of mental and physical illness comes from our thought life rather than the environment and genes.

John 8:44 describes how Satan is the father of lies. We have to stop believing Satan's lies and cast them out.

Philippians 4:8 says, "Whatever is true, whatever is noble, whatever is right, whatever is pure, whatever is lovely, whatever is admirable—if anything is excellent or praiseworthy—think about such things."

In *Switch On Your Brain*, chapter 5, Caroline Leaf also says: "By following this perfect advice from God's Word, you can bring back the balance between the default mode network (DMN) and the task positive network (TPN)." I highly recommend her book as it explains further what this means.

Does God want us to think about whatever is bad or negative? No. God tells us to think all good thoughts, so the minute we have a negative thought, we need to know it's not from God. We need to refresh our minds. Hit the delete button. Change the channel.

I've heard it said that attitude determines altitude, and it's really true. We flourish in positive atmospheres and wither in negative ones. I know I would not be where I am today if I hadn't partnered with the Paul Mitchell company. Their very culture includes a consistent message of "forward focus," meaning there is always a solution to every problem. Getting stuck and negative about a situation kills our creativity and production.

Years ago, we hired a woman at one of our schools who was talented and qualified for her position but she had a bit of a negative attitude. Every time I spoke to her, she shared her drama with me. There was always something negative happening in her life. I mentioned it to the school leaders but because she was helpful and always the first to assist during challenges, they kept her on. That eventually backfired when she caused a big ruckus in our schools and we had to terminate her. We should have done it a long time ago, because it was the best thing we did for us and for her. A year later she messaged me to apologize: she had turned her life around. If we had released her many years earlier, she might have turned her life around sooner. The lesson we learned from that experience: don't be held hostage by people on your teams. Do what's best for your culture, and ultimately that will be best for them, too.

Since then I've made it a non-negotiable in hiring that we will never hire anyone who is even a little bit negative. There is nothing negative about God: He is always positive and if we want to raise our altitude in life we have to be the same way. I love Colossians 3:2 (AMP): "Set your mind and keep focused habitually on the things above (the heavenly things), not on things that are on the earth (which have only temporal value)." God is literally telling us to set our minds and keep them set on staying positive.

In my book, *Be Amazing*, I talk about changing the channel by changing our thoughts and being around positive people. For a long time, I could only be around people who were 100 percent positive. I'm very energy sensitive and negative energy rubbed off on me. Unlike people who enjoy negative and drama-filled TV shows, I literally have to grab the remote and change the channel. Most days I turn off the TV and sit in silence or read a book.

POWER STATEMENTS

In *Be Amazing*, I also wrote about getting ice in your veins. My son Justin was a high school and college football quarterback, and I'll never forget what his coach said after Justin messed up several times: "Do you know what your problem is? You gotta get ice in your veins. You gotta get that mental toughness." For me, the best way to get mental toughness in my life is to build power statements that mean something to me from God's Word. Proverbs 23:7 (TPT) says, "For as he thinks within himself, so is he." Our brains are designed to respond to our minds, and power statements are a great way to retrain our brains.

The most powerful thing God has shown me through the years is to meditate nonstop on His Word: to memorize and repeat it over and over. 2 Corinthians 10:5 tells us we can capture "every thought and insist that it bow in obedience" to Jesus Christ. On her website, Christian author and speaker Joyce Meyer has a great handout called "List of Confessions by Joyce Meyer." As I studied scripture after scripture, something told me, "You need to memorize this."

Unfortunately, memorizing didn't come easily to me. I had so much anxiety and frustration, but God said, "No. There's nothing to worry about

ever." That's what Philippians 4:6–7 tells us in
The Passion Translation (TPT) of the Bible:

> Don't be pulled in different
> directions or worried about a thing.
> Be saturated in prayer throughout
> each day, offering your faith-filled
> requests before God with overflowing
> gratitude. Tell Him every detail of
> your life, then God's wonderful
> peace that transcends human
> understanding, will make the answers
> known to you through Jesus Christ.

At the point where I said, "God, help me! I can't memorize your scripture; it's just not sinking in," God said, "That's okay. You can get creative." So I turned the verses into power statements that I could remember. You'll see them at the end of this chapter. They've transformed my life. Feel free to steal them or come up with your own.

In 2013, while I was trying to memorize the scriptures, I was diagnosed with a precancerous lesion. I have to tell you, I had so much peace about it. I was actually joy-filled and I said, "I'm going to be able to change lives." And guess what happened? I've been able to save lives. I am now an education ambassador for the nonprofit organization Bright Pink. I lead thirty-minute workshops and train women to prevent breast and ovarian cancer.

How good is God! I remember saying those scriptures over and again. I was giggling to myself—yes, actually giggling—as I went into the operating room. My husband was pale as he headed to the waiting area but the doctor said to me, "You are such a happy person, aren't you?" I was thinking, "It's just God." I went under anesthesia, woke up, and within four weeks I was fine. It was an incredible surgery; a piece of cake. Many women have told me it's the worst surgery they've ever had, but I know my strength came from God and from memorizing scripture after scripture.

We can be overwhelmed by setbacks or energized by the opportunities they bring. With crisis comes opportunity! I recently listened to a podcast and the speaker said something so profound. Unfortunately, I don't recall who it was but I truly believe the message: "Things don't happen TO you, they happen THROUGH you, FOR other people." The worst event in our lives often prepares us for the greatest assignment in our lives.

Throughout my marriage with Bryan, I've tended to be meaner to him than anyone else, taking my frustrations out on the person I love the most. One day as I was angry at him and lashing out, God stopped me in my tracks. I told myself, "Wait a minute. You teach an online Bible study with your husband called Leadership Begins at Home. Shouldn't you be a great leader at home?" So I kept repeating this power statement to myself: "Adversity reveals character. Pass the test." And I'll tell you, it worked. We know who the power is, and the power source.

Tina's Power Statements

Here's the list of power statements that transformed my life. Compare them to the scripture listed next to them. God gives me a new power statement almost every day from His Word. You can use mine if they hit home with you or make up some of your own.

- There's nothing to worry about ever. (Philippians 4:6)
- Failure is my friend. (Philippians 3:13–14)
- Press on! (Philippians 3:14)
- 20 seconds of courage (2 Timothy 1:7)
- Do it now. (Proverbs 6:4–11)
- No weapon formed against me shall prosper. (Isaiah 54:17)
- Adversity reveals character. (Romans 5:3–4)
- Pass the test! (2 Chronicles 15:7)
- Inhale confidence, exhale doubt. (Philippians 4:13)
- Sow and grow. (Matthew 13:44–46)
- I am quick to listen and slow to speak. (James 1:19–20)
- Pray, don't say. (Psalm 141:3)

Tina's "I Am" Statements

- I am complete in Him who is the head of all principality and power. (Colossians 2:10)
- I am free from the law of sin and death. (Romans 8:2)
- I am holy and without blame before Him in love. (Ephesians 1:4; 1 Peter 1:16)

- I have the mind of Christ. (1 Corinthians 2:16; Philippians 2:5)
- I have the peace of God that passes all understanding. (Philippians 4:7)
- I have received the power of the Holy Spirit to lay hands on the sick and see them recover, to cast out demons, to speak with new tongues. I have power over all the power of the enemy, and nothing shall by any means harm me. (Mark 16:17–18; Luke 10:17–19)
- I can do all things through Christ Jesus. (Philippians 4:13)
- I am a doer of the word and blessed in my actions. (James 1:22–25)
- I am joint heir with Christ. (Romans 8:17)
- I am more than a conqueror through Him who loves me. (Romans 8:37)
- I am the temple of the Holy Spirit; I am not my own. (1 Corinthians 6:19)
- I am the head and not the tail, I am above only and not beneath. (Deuteronomy 28:13)
- I am the light of the world. (Matthew 5:14)
- I am forgiven of all sins and washed in the blood. (Ephesians 1:7)
- I am an ambassador for Christ. (2 Corinthians 5:20)

UNLOCK THE POWER OF PRAISE

Something else God has been teaching me this past year is how to unlock the power of praise. I've been working through Dr. Caroline Leaf's online "21-Day

Brain Detox Plan" guide, and it's amazing what just three minutes a day can do. She recommends that we spend the first three minutes of the day thanking, praising, and worshipping God. My mind is starting to believe what the spirit already knows: that God wired us for love and we have to capture every negative thought to live our purpose—which is to love!

To get yourself into that space, try meditating on these verses.

31 Days to Get Your Praise On

I put together a sample **31 Days to Get Your Praise On**, or you can create your own, with the scriptures of your choice. Setting aside time to focus on scripture each day is a great way to learn how to pray them. When you read a scripture verse, pinpoint something within it that you can praise God for and repeat it throughout the day. The following are my "pinpoints" from the selected scriptures.

Day 1: Psalm 145 (TPT): You can read the entire psalm as a prayer and praise to God or just focus on the first verse, which really spoke to me. My Day 1 pinpoint: Lord, my heart explodes with praise to you. Now and forever I bow in worship, my king and my God.

Day 2: Psalm 103:22 (TPT): I bless and praise you, my Lord, with my whole heart.

Day 3: Romans 8:28 (TPT): I praise you, my Lord, that every single detail of my life is continually woven together to fit into your perfect plans.

Day 4: Matthew 6:14–15 (TPT): Lord, I praise you for your forgiveness of all my wrong doings.

Day 5: 2 Timothy 2:13 (TPT): I praise you, Lord, for your faithfulness.

Day 6: Revelation 4:8 (TPT): Holy, holy, holy are you, Lord God almighty.

Day 7: Matthew 11:28–29 (TPT): I praise you for your gentleness and how easy it is to please you. I praise you for refreshing me continually and for rest in you.

Day 8: Ephesians 3:20 (TPT): I praise you for your mighty power working in me to achieve infinitely more than my greatest requests, my most unbelievable dreams, and my wildest imagination. I praise you for your miraculous power constantly energizing me.

Day 9: Psalm 150 (TPT): Lord, I praise you for your magnificent greatness.

Day 10: Psalm 119:171 (TPT): I praise you for all that you have taught me.

Day 11: Read Psalm 95:2 (TPT): Lord, I shout for joy for your greatness.

Day 12: Psalm 28:7 (TPT): Lord, I jump for joy and burst forth with ecstatic passionate praise for you in my life.

Day 13: James 1:5–6 (TPT): Lord, I praise you for generously giving me wisdom.

Day 14: Psalm 66:20 (TPT): I praise you for always hearing my prayers.

Day 15: Psalm 42:8 (TPT): I praise you for your promises of love pouring over me all day and all night long.

Day 16: 1 Thessalonians 5:16–17 (TPT): I praise you for joy and that I can constantly pray to you.

Day 17: Psalm 95:2 (TPT): Lord, I will not withhold my praise to you. I shout for joy over your greatness.

Day 18: Psalm 23 (TPT): I praise you that your goodness and love pursue me all the days of my life, and when my life is over I will be in your glorious presence.

Day 19: 2 Samuel 22:2–4 (AMPC): I praise you that you are my rock, my fortress, my deliverer, my shield, the horn of my salvation, my stronghold, my refuge, my savior.

Day 20: Genesis 22:13–15 (AMPC): I praise you for being my provider.

Day 21: Exodus 17:15–16 (AMPC): I praise you for being my banner.

Day 22: Judge 6:24 (AMPC): I praise you for being my peace.

Day 23: Daniel 4:34 (AMPC): I praise and honor and glorify you, Lord who lives forever.

Day 24: Jonah 2:1–6 (AMPC): I praise you for a life spared from the pit and corruption.

Day 25: Luke 1:46–55 (TPT): I praise you for favor, blessings, working mighty miracles, and your mighty power.

Day 26: 2 Chronicles 5:13 (AMPC): I praise you for mercy and that your loving kindness endures forever.

Day 27: Psalm 95:6–9 (TPT): I bow down before you, mighty God, my majestic maker.

Day 28: Psalm 99:5 (TPT): I exalt you, Lord my God, face down before your glory throne, for you are great and holy.

Day 29: Psalm 103:1 (TPT): I praise you with my whole heart, my whole life, my innermost being. I bow in wonder and love before you, my holy God.

Day 30: Psalm 68:4–6 (TPT): I praise you for being my father, my champion, my true family, and for prosperity.

Day 31: Psalm 98:4 (TPT): Lord, I shout out your praises with joy.

STEP 2 EXERCISE: SCRIPTURES FOR UNCOMMON THOUGHTS

The following scriptures support the idea that uncommon people have uncommon thoughts. As you read them, jot down some notes about how each one applies to you.

- **Colossians 3:1–2**: "Since, then, you have been raised with Christ, set your hearts on things above, where Christ is, seated at the right hand of God. Set your minds on things above, not on earthly things."

- **Romans 12:2 (ESV)**: "Do not be conformed to this world, but be transformed by the renewal of your mind, that by testing you may discern what is the will of God, what is good and acceptable and perfect."

- **Romans 8:5 (AMP)**: "For those who are living according to the flesh set their minds on the things of the flesh [which gratify the body], but those who are living according to the Spirit, [set their minds on] the things of the Spirit [His will and purpose]."

- **2 Timothy 1:7**: "For the Spirit God gave us does not make us timid, but gives us power, love and self-discipline."

BE UNCOMMON

- **Matthew 15:11 (MSG)**: "Listen, and take this to heart. It's not what you swallow that pollutes your life, but what you vomit up."

- **1 John 4:4 (ESV)**: "Little children, you are from God and have overcome them, for He who is in you is greater than He who is in the world."

- **Luke 10:27 (AMP)**: "You shall love the Lord your God with all your heart, and with all your soul, and with all your strength, and with all your mind; and your neighbor as yourself."

Now add some of your own favorite verses here.

Step

3

UNCOMMON FRIENDS

Brianna:

Proverbs 13:20 (TPT) says, "If you want to grow in wisdom, spend time with the wise." I truly believe this is what helped our family along our journey. We have incredible mentors and surround ourselves with amazing people. It's amazing when God puts people in our lives and opens the door for relationships. I think about how God connected me with Ken Paves, one of the greatest celebrity stylists in the world. That connection opened many doors for me and my career. Ultimately God's purpose was that our family would own businesses to change lives and help people find their purpose and God-given identity. It's been that way since day one, and we watched as God aligned us with the right people at the right time on our journey.

It's also amazing how God sometimes makes the most unlikely connections, leading us to people we never thought possible, to bring us to the next level or promotion. We can accomplish very little as a self-made man or woman, compared to what God can do as a supernatural God. He is the God of the impossible. When we let our requests be made known to God, He WILL give us the desires of our hearts. Philippians 4:6–7 and Psalm 37:4 let us know that God can open doors that we can't open on our own. He goes beyond our natural networking circles to bring us into the plan and purposes He spoke over us before we were even born.

Tina:

I'm blessed to include my uncommon family members among my uncommon friends. Bryan and I have been married for over thirty years and I still like to call him "my boyfriend." (We have to keep it fresh, ladies! But that's another book.) Our incredible children, Brianna and Justin, are in their mid-twenties now, and I always say they raised us. I remember one time when Justin was three years old and I was cooking at the stove. He said something so spiritual that I looked at him and said, "Justin, you're my little pastor!" When Brianna was in high school, she started attending a church that had an amazing youth group and Justin soon got involved, too. That was the start for both of them in constantly seeking a deeper relationship with God and a knowledge of spirituality. They both had so much more confidence than I ever did growing up.

Today, Brianna and Justin keep learning, growing, and teaching me about God's truths; they've opened my eyes to greater understanding and a stronger presence of the Holy Spirit in my life. They've both been exposed to many great pastors over the years, and they both have completed ministry courses through their churches. They've introduced me to several pastors who have given me a fresh perspective on God's love for humankind and my ability to create heaven on earth. Both Brianna and Justin have an incredible inner circle of friends who truly love the Lord and grow their spirituality on a consistent basis. I'm over fifty years old now and I've had a surface-level Christianity over the years, but my hunger has grown from watching their growth, seeing their confidence, and knowing they have a God plan—not just a good plan—to fulfill.

UNDERSTAND YOUR VALUE

Tina:

After the salon walkout I mentioned earlier, I kept telling myself that I didn't know what I was doing. But Ken Paves believed in me, and my husband and daughter believe in me. My son believes in me and frequently tells me that I'm his biggest hero. My business partners Winn Claybaugh and John Paul DeJoria and their team believe in me, and there is rarely a moment that they don't tell me so. Sometimes we just have to borrow people's belief in us.

In my book *Be Amazing*, I listed several steps to success, and I truly believe these next steps can help you have uncommon friends.

First and foremost, you must understand your value.

BE UNCOMMON

I spent a lot of years speaking negativity and doom and gloom over myself. As a child, I was called names like buck-toothed beaver, ugly, four-eyes, and stupid. I started to believe those lies and let them sink deep into my soul, and I think that took me off my purpose.

Children are born with such confidence. They want to do big things; they want to change the world. Without hesitation, children will dream about the wonderful things they'll do, places they'll go, and superheroes they'll become. But then life happens: the wrong people get into our lives and speak lies over us and we start to believe them.

Until I learned about Jesus dying for me when I was eighteen, I didn't know how valuable I was. Until then, I didn't realize that I was God's masterpiece. I want to encourage you to understand that you, too, are God's masterpiece.

Amazingly enough, years later, I married my husband who speaks life back into me. Remember I said I struggled with depression and negative, defeating thoughts? Not Bryan. He believed in me. He told me daily how beautiful I am and how I could change the world. He always supported me and cheered me on with every endeavor I undertook. It's important to surround yourself with people who believe in you and root for you. In fact, that's the third step to being uncommon.

Sometimes understanding your value is a matter of telling yourself over and over and over, "I am valuable." Look in the mirror while you say it. It will feel a bit awkward at first.

Most of the time I look in the mirror and think, *Oh dear, you need some Botox.* But then I hit the delete button and speak God's truth over myself. Try writing it on your mirror, or on your computer. (I know some people who write positive messages all over their mirrors.) Once in a while I put sticky notes with "I am ___" statements.

I love Luke 12:6–7 (NLT). I'm in the hair industry, so of course I love this one:

> What is the price of five sparrows—two copper coins? Yet God does not forget a single one of them. And the very hairs on your head are all numbered. So don't be afraid; you are more valuable to God than a whole flock of sparrows.

It seems impossible that God knows how many hairs are on our heads, but it shows how important we are to Him.

What more can God do to show us that He loves us relentlessly and infinitely and how valuable we are to Him than the one hundred verses throughout the Bible about Christ dying for us? Romans 5:8 says it all: "But God demonstrates His own love for us in this: While we were still sinners, Christ died for us." Take a moment to meditate on this verse and thank God for dying for you. *You are valuable!*

Still don't feel valuable? Sift through the Bible and find the one hundred verses about Christ dying for you and read them until you truly know how valuable you are.

This first step toward having uncommon friends can't be skipped, because when you truly know your value you'll be in a place to constantly surround yourself with people who value you as well. There is power in proximity! Always be on the lookout for new mentors and new uncommon friends who can help take you to the next level spiritually and professionally.

Brianna:

In partnership with God, we live from a place of rest. A healthy identity says, "I don't have to perform to obtain rest or value." When we understand our identity, we value ourselves. And when we understand that we have value, we put value on our purpose. Everyone has purpose; if you're breathing, you have purpose. Life is a journey, and when we give God permission to invade our journey, our purpose gets a whole lot bigger, our convictions stronger, and joy overtakes us. We were designed to have an uncommon life with uncommon plans and uncommon friends.

Proverbs 21:21 (TPT) reminds us that "The lovers of God who chase after righteousness will find all their dreams come true: an abundant life drenched with favor and a fountain that overflows with satisfaction."

The more we spend time with God and get to know Him, the more we understand ourselves and the value that we have. The enemy will convince us that we don't have value, and what he cannot take from us he will convince us to give away. He even puts people in our lives who convince us we don't have value. The devil is a liar. The Bible says the thief comes to kill, steal, and destroy. His top job is to get our eyes off Jesus, who made us worthy. Jesus paid the ultimate price by dying on the cross so we would be seen as faultless and blameless in the eyes of God the Father. He took our place so we could be in right standing with the Father. Think about that for a minute. You are valuable. Your life has value. Your purpose has value. You weren't an accident. God knows you and loves you as you are.

STALK VISIONARIES AND THE POWER OF PROXIMITY

Tina:

My favorite verse in the Bible is Proverbs 27:17, "As iron sharpens iron, so one person sharpens another." I would not be where I am today if I hadn't gone up to shake hands with all the amazing mentors and business partners I have.

When I say "stalk visionaries," it's just a funny statement to get you moving. Find someone you want to be like, tell them how grateful you are for them, and ask them to mentor you. If you're afraid, do it afraid. Go after them like your life depends on it. That's the power of proximity.

Ask yourself these questions: Who inspires me? Who is honest with me? And whose skills complement mine? My mentor, John C. Maxwell, calls it the "who-luck" principle: who would you be lucky to meet or have in your life? When you can answer those questions, your proximity will change because you are who you hang with, whether you like or not.

Who you are is who you will attract in your life. If you're frustrated with the people in your life, look in the mirror. It took so much transformation in myself to start drawing the right people in my business—the right partners, the right staff, and the right clients.

In the leadership classes and masterminds I lead, people always ask me how to fix their staff. It's funny because you don't have to change your people; all you have to do is fix and change yourself. It's so important to get around like-minded people who will lift you up and help you through your challenges.

Brianna:

Two of my favorite quotes are "Whatever you fear, do next" and "Do it afraid."

I'm actually very introspective and shy. Given the opportunity, I would rather stay at home than go anywhere. At times, it's good to process and be self-aware, but it can also be a weakness that holds me back from opportunities. Nothing good ever happens in our comfort zone. I think God likes to stretch us and pull us out of our comfort so we'll learn to fully rely on Him, because that's where miracles happen. When we push past our fears and just say yes, we learn to let go, trust, and fly!

When I first had the desire to teach cosmetology to human trafficking victims, nothing happened for five years. I was waiting for God to move, but I sometimes wonder if He's waiting for us to move! When I heard my pastor talking about Angel House in Nepal, something in my spirit jumped and that was it. I emailed everyone connected with them and said, "Let me get involved with this! Let me add value to this mission!" Three years later, we have trained over one hundred girls in cosmetology and opened a beautiful safe home for them, where hundreds will be rescued, trained, and healed.

As 2 Corinthians 1:20 (TPT) says, "For all of God's promises find their 'yes' of fulfillment in Him. And as His 'yes' and our 'amen' ascend to God, we bring Him glory!" Saying yes to God means saying no to fear.

Opportunity happens when we take a leap and find our wings on the way down. God has promises for you. His yes is for you. Will you agree with Him, and say amen?

WHO CAN YOU ADD TO YOUR CIRCLE? WHO CAN YOU STALK?

Tina:

As I mentioned earlier, John C. Maxwell talked about "who-luck," meaning who are you lucky to meet?

God lines up people in our lives for a reason. I'm amazed at the people I've met who have altered my life forever. My husband Bryan was my first who-luck—he lived downstairs from me over thirty years ago, and thank God he asked my roommate if I had a boyfriend. Next were Winn Claybaugh and John Paul DeJoria, my Paul Mitchell business partners who believed in me. Salon owner Kelly Cardenas taught me so much about salon business and success in life. John C. Maxwell helped me become a better leader so I could expand my businesses. Pastor Tim Storey came into our family's life and my son moved to California to work with him and start an online fitness business. Another who-luck in my life is Sue, who provides cleaning services at one of our businesses. Sue has taught me how to be present for people and I'm so lucky to have her in my life. My dog Sammy is another who-luck in my life; he taught me how to slow down this past year. This list could keep going!

Who's your who-luck? Who would you be lucky to meet? Are you willing to take risks and get into position to meet your next who-luck? To attract and learn from a who-luck, the most important attributes you can have are to be humble, coachable, and teachable. Observe. Ask questions. Listen.

Brianna:

In the kingdom of God, nothing happens by coincidence so I truly believe that God puts people in our lives. It's those "too good to be true moments" when we meet the right person or happen to be in the right place at the right time.

When we're operating in our purpose and flowing in what God has for us, God will go beyond our networking circle and beyond our natural circle of influence to bring divine moments of connection with people. That's the God we serve. He is so good and so much bigger than we can possibly imagine.

One example for me happened many years ago, when my mom signed up for the John Maxwell team. A year after she signed up they asked if she knew a makeup artist who could help the team and of course she said, "Yes, my daughter."

I had no idea what I was getting involved in, but seven years later I'm still doing the makeup and makeovers for John Maxwell's events. By doing the makeup for all of the speakers, I've met many influential people, including top leaders around the world, heads of companies like Chick-fil-A CEO Dan Cathy, motivational speaker and author Nick Vujicic, and many more.

It's an honor to spend time with John Maxwell and these amazing leaders, some of whom have been my who-lucks. When John Maxwell Team President Paul Martinelli asked me about my passions and goals, I shared with him that my heart was to help girls who have been rescued from sex trafficking in Nepal. I told him about my ministry there and about building a safe home for girls who have been rescued and training them in cosmetology. I was leaving for my first trip to Nepal in one month, but I was financially at the lowest I've ever been because I had done three mission trips in the past year and funded them by myself.

I was having a whiny moment with God, "Why am I doing this? I'm emptying my bank account for you. What is the point of all this?" I prayed. When I told

Paul this he immediately said, "I don't know why but I feel like God wants me to tithe to your mission and what you're doing in Nepal." He told me how much he wanted to give, and it was the exact amount to the dollar that I needed for the trip.

At that moment, God reminded me that He would always provide for me and always take care of me, if I just surrender and keep saying yes to Him. That was the moment I knew there's no coincidence in the kingdom of God. He sees every worry, every anxious thought, and He says to lay them at His feet. God will always provide for us in ways we never thought possible because that's just who He is. When we follow God and walk with Him, He aligns us with our purpose and brings the right people at the right time.

Winn Claybaugh (Dean of Paul Mitchell Schools), the Andrew Gomez Dream Foundation, and Paul Mitchell Pro Tools provided $16,000 worth of equipment for the girls to learn cosmetology. Winn was also my who-luck in making this dream happen.

After I got home from Nepal, we spent the next two years fundraising to build a training center and safe home. The need was $100,000. All of the money has been raised by many generous people and fundraisers that raised one dollar at a time. Nothing is impossible with God. Make your requests known to Him and He will give you the desires of your heart.

STEP 3 EXERCISE: SCRIPTURES FOR UNCOMMON FRIENDS

Here are some scriptures to encourage you on your journey of attracting uncommon friends. Go through the verses and write down how you can specifically apply them to your life.

- **Proverbs 13:20 (ESV)**: "Whoever walks with the wise becomes wise, but the companion of fools will suffer harm."

- **Proverbs 27:17 (AMP)**: "As iron sharpens iron, so one man sharpens [and influences] another [through discussion]."

- **Ecclesiastes 4:9–10 (NLT)**: "Two people are better off than one, for they can help each other succeed. If one person falls, the other can reach out and help. But someone who falls alone is in real trouble."

- **1 Thessalonians 5:11**: "Therefore encourage one another and build each other up, just as in fact you are doing."

- **1 Corinthians 15:33 (ESV)**: "Do not be deceived: 'Bad company ruins good morals.'"

- **Proverbs 18:24 (NLT)**: "There are 'friends' who destroy each other, but a real friend sticks closer than a brother."

- **Proverbs 12:26**: "The righteous choose their friends carefully, but the way of the wicked leads them astray."

- **James 4:4 (AMP)**: "You adulteresses [disloyal sinners—flirting with the world and breaking your vow to God]! Do you not know that being the world's friend [that is, loving the things of the world] is being God's enemy? So whoever chooses to be a friend of the world makes himself an enemy of God."

- **Proverbs 27:9 (NLT)**: "The heartfelt counsel of a friend is as sweet as perfume and incense."

- **Hebrews 10:24–25 (ESV)**: "And let us consider how to stir up one another to love and good works, not neglecting to meet together, as is the habit of some, but encouraging one another, and all the more as you see the Day drawing near."

What other verses can you add?

UNCOMMON DISCIPLINE

Tina:

The last, and to me one of the most important steps to being uncommon, is having uncommon discipline in all areas of our lives. We are personal representatives of Jesus Christ and we need to put on behavior that represents Him. We not only have the mind of Christ but we have the spirit of God in us and we don't have the privilege of acting like everyone else. We are aliens from a foreign planet. We don't belong here; we're just passing through. Our purpose is to represent God and bring other people to Him through our godly behavior.

> If in fact you have [really] heard Him and have been taught by Him, just as truth is in Jesus [revealed in His life and personified in Him], that, regarding your previous way of life, you put off your old self [completely discard your former nature], which

is being corrupted through deceitful desires, and be *continually* renewed in the spirit of your mind [having a fresh, untarnished mental and spiritual attitude], and put on the new self [the regenerated and renewed nature], created in God's image, [godlike] in the righteousness and holiness of the truth [living in a way that expresses to God your gratitude for your salvation].
Ephesians 4:21–24 (AMP)

What I love MOST about this verse is "living in a way that expresses to God your *gratitude* for your salvation." Let that sink deep down: live in a way… that expresses to God…your *gratitude* for your salvation. The minute I get off track is the minute I've lost my gratitude for Jesus dying for me.

Have you seen the movie *The Promise*? It was one of the hardest movies for me to watch because it vividly depicts the brutality of Christ's beating and crucifixion—you can feel the actual emotions of how much Jesus loves you. So if you're thinking, "No, Tina, He didn't die for me," or "No, Tina, I don't 'feel' like God died for me," then watch the movie—over and over again, if necessary. You will sob and break down in pure joy after that movie, and never again want to live in a way that doesn't honor Him.

I remember when I told a friend that I couldn't bear to watch what they did to Christ in the movie. My friend told me point blank to watch it, because I needed to feel the emotions of how much God loves me. When we know how much He loves us, we will never again devalue ourselves or other people, not even our enemies. The more I concentrate on those emotions, the easier it is to stop taking things personally, such as when someone devalues me or speaks poorly of me or to me. It's absolute *freedom* in this life, and you need to try it on!

Because of gratitude for my salvation, I've also found freedom from repeatedly reliving my past or past bad experiences like I used to do. 2 Corinthians 5:17 (TPT) says, "Now, if anyone is enfolded into Christ, he has become an entirely new creation. All that is related to the old order has vanished. Behold, everything is fresh and new." This means we can stop carrying old baggage and wearing those old clothes. We can drop the negative attitudes. The past. Depression. Fear. Victim mentality. Jesus died so we could swap those old clothes for resurrection clothes.

Remember I said that when I was sixteen years old I wrote my family a suicide note? I walked in and out of depression from age sixteen to my late twenties. I hid it well from my family, but my husband knew it only too well. He was the brunt of my complaining. He told me that when we were dating, I was sad a lot. I shared with him my deepest, darkest pain and then one day I was completely free of it all. Now I am one of the most joy-filled people you'll ever meet. I'm rarely without a smile on my face. It's amazing what God can do and the freedom we can have once we truly know how much He loves us.

Brianna:

If you don't stand for something, you will fall for anything. To have uncommon discipline, you have to stand for something. You get to decide who you want to be; not your parents, not your circumstances, not your bank account. You get to choose who you want to be. It was a powerful moment when I had this revelation. I am responsible for my own life. I am responsible to choose who I want to be.

God created us to have free will. He wants us to choose Him. He wants us to choose to participate with the purpose He has already spoken over us. We have a choice. You have a choice. How exciting that we serve a God who has a plan and a purpose for us before we were even born. The Bible says that when we were in our mother's womb, He knew who we were. God, the creator of the universe and of you and I, is asking, "Do you want to participate with your free will?"

Having that strong awareness of who I am came at a young age because the Lord had begun to speak into me my identity. Yes, I was raised in a Christian home and had an amazing foundation built, but when we enter our teens, we start to become our own person and begin to ask, "Who am I, what am I supposed to do with my life, what was I created for?" Growing in maturity and growing in relationship with God takes uncommon discipline. We may even go through seasons of isolation to allow God to mature a dream in us and develop us. As believers we all have a new nature. When we accept Christ into our hearts and believe in Him, we get a new nature; we are born again. But we also get a new identity. To understand it, we have to have an intimate relationship with the one who created us.

Before I met my husband Corey, I had just come out of a toxic relationship. I had dated the same guy for eight years. We had a roller coaster relationship through high school, and it became more serious as we entered into adulthood and considered each other for marriage. I loved him; at least, I thought it was love. We grew up together and we were comfortable together. We fought hard for our relationship to work, but we both knew it wouldn't. I convinced myself, like so many people do, that he would be my husband. I was stubborn and I had already given him so much of myself that I believed my heart was unredeemable.

One night while I was still in high school, God gave me a very specific dream. I was holding a box and crying hysterically as I gave the box to God. The box was filled with dirt, dust, and bones, and it represented death. Laughing, God took the box and filled it with love. Then He gave me a new box, wrapped in beautiful paper with a red bow. I tried to open it but God said, "No, don't open it until I tell you." I was seventeen years old when I had this dream. I knew it was from God and I knew it was about my unhealthy, ungodly relationship.

Yet I chose to push it aside, to justify it, to ignore it. John 10:10 (ESV) says, "The thief comes only to steal and kill and destroy. I [God] came that they may have life and have it abundantly."

What the enemy can't steal from you, he will convince you to give away. I was giving away my purity, my heart, my emotions. I was settling for what felt good, what felt comfortable. I was stubborn, I was filled with pride, and nothing and no one was going to break apart this relationship, even though deep down I knew God had more, He had better, He had a man picked out for me. I knew my boyfriend wasn't my Plan A. No, he was Plan B and, honestly, I was okay with that. I liked Plan B. It was comfortable.

When the relationship ended I was crushed, heartbroken, and at a very low point. I knew what I had to do: I surrendered my love life back to God. I prayed that day, "God, I've given every part of my life to you except this one area. I've wanted to control it on my own, and today I choose to surrender. I give you my love life because I want you to choose my husband. I give up all control," and that was it. Overwhelming peace flooded my heart.

I really felt like I was supposed to give the next year to God. I knew He wanted to heal a lot of areas of my heart. I would have to walk through some hard stuff: forgiving my ex-boyfriend, forgiving myself, breaking off soul ties. It wasn't going to be easy, the temptation was there—oh yes, it was. Four months later I almost went back; it took everything in me not to. I was fighting a spiritual battle. During that time, I had the revelation that my choice would impact generations after me; that if I gave into my emotions and feelings of "I'll always love him," I would be choosing not only my destiny but that of my children and my children's children. I had to choose wisdom. In hard moments, God gives us the grace to choose wisdom over our emotions.

Three weeks after the breakup, I moved to a new city and started getting more involved at my church. At a young adult service, I met Corey. He was intriguing and handsome. You couldn't miss him—he's almost seven feet tall. He was standing next to me, worshipping God like no one else was in the room.

I wasn't looking for a relationship. I was looking for friends, a new circle, a new environment. He kept showing up at different events and we would casually talk. One Sunday, he sat near me in church, and after church I invited him and four other friends to my parents' boat. He became very flirtatious, and even though I enjoyed the attention, I told him right away that I wasn't looking for a relationship right now, that for the next year I was surrendering my love life to Jesus and working on myself. He replied, "That's good because I'm moving to Bulgaria next week for nine months to play professional basketball."

The next day I agreed to go on one date, just as friends. He was different. In our short time together I heard the Lord say, "This is your husband." It shocked me and overwhelmed me, but I felt an incredible peace, so I trusted the Lord.

For the next nine months, we stayed in contact and built an incredible foundation and friendship. We were falling in love. This was the type of love story only God could write, and we both felt so much peace. Corey honored the commitment I had made with the Lord and didn't pursue me or pressure me until my "one year" was over. Five months after dating, we were engaged to be married. On July 1, 2018, we celebrated our one-year anniversary.

From a very young age, I've known what I wanted to do in my life. I graduated from our cosmetology school before I graduated high school. I was licensed in Michigan and Florida and went on to get my instructor's license so I could be an educator. After six years of working in our Paul Mitchell schools, we had the opportunity to partner with Ken Paves. He had a salon in Michigan and wanted to partner with us! I became a salon owner at age twenty-three. Even though I was in a leadership role and had been groomed for business since I was sixteen, I learned discipline in the trenches. You have to go through the trenches, you have to go through the hard stuff to really develop leadership.

One year after taking over the salon, we lost our entire team to a walkout. Without warning, they all plotted to move to another salon and take their clients with them. In that low moment for us as leaders, we all looked in the mirror and said, "It's my fault." Then we picked ourselves up and reinvented ourselves. The walkout ended up being the biggest blessing in disguise because we hired brand-new stylists right out of our cosmetology schools. They already knew the Paul Mitchell culture, which is love, giving back, and positivity. You can always grow people's technical skills, but it's harder to train culture. We hire people first. We want our team to have a job they love and to feel like their purpose is being fulfilled. Our team is thriving because we truly are a family. We have created a culture in our business of love and teamwork. Our Paul Mitchell The Salon is expanding to The Salon Naples and The Salon Fullerton, and our goal is to someday open a thousand salons. It may not happen in our lifetime, but we know God gave us that dream so we are saying yes and amen to that promise!

SEE YOURSELF AS GOD SEES YOU

Tina:

One day God said to me, "There is nothing you can do, Tina, to make me love you less. And there is nothing you can do to make me love you more." Are you hearing this? If you're thinking, "No, Tina, that's just for you, that's not for me," No! Don't believe those lies. Let this message get into your soul. Do what you have to do to truly know God's love for you. You owe it to Him, yourself, and everyone around you. You need to see yourself as God sees you.

If you will see yourself as God sees you, you will become what He says you are.

> For God did not give us a spirit of timidity *or* cowardice *or* fear, but [He has given us a spirit] of power and of love and of sound judgment *and* personal discipline [abilities that result in a calm, well-balanced mind and self-control].
> 2 Timothy 1:7 (AMP)

If God says we have a spirit of discipline, then we have a spirit for discipline! God sees you as you can be, not as you are, so just agree with Him and it will come to pass. Wow! Let that sink in. Stop what you are doing and agree with Him that you have uncommon discipline.

> And we all, with unveiled face, *continually* seeing as in a mirror the glory of the Lord, are *progressively* being transformed into His image from [one degree of] glory to [even more] glory, which comes from the Lord, [who is] the Spirit.
> 2 Corinthians 3:18 (AMP)

> Whenever, though, they turn to face God as Moses did, God removes the veil and there they are—face-to-face! They suddenly recognize that God is a living, personal presence, not a piece of chiseled stone. And when God is personally present, a living Spirit, that old, constricting legislation is recognized as obsolete. We're free of it! All of us! Nothing between us and God, our faces shining with the brightness of His face. And so we are transfigured much like the Messiah, our lives gradually becoming brighter and more beautiful as God enters our lives and we become like Him.
> 2 Corinthians 3:16–18 (MSG)

Let that sink in. What I love the most about The Message's version of this verse is the sentence, "God is a living, personal presence."

Brianna:

The Bible verse found in 2 Corinthians 3:18 talks about moving from glory to glory. This is such a powerful truth because it's actually a belief system about our own identity. What does that mean for us? It means the God of the universe wants you to see yourself made in *His* image. Where the spirit of the Lord is, there is liberty, all veils removed. Once we see Jesus, we see ourselves made perfect because of what He did for us on the cross. Moving from His glory to another glory means the more we understand our identity in Him, the more we move into deeper revelation that only gets stronger and sweeter, and life only gets better because now we can clearly see. The real secret to discovering the glory of God is falling in love. Every day, falling deeper in love with Jesus. His love has no depths, no bounds, and is endless for you.

God doesn't want to be this religious thing we do on a Sunday morning. He wants to be part of every detail of our lives. He is an intimate God who desires nothing more than relationship with us. He wants to take us into the glory of knowing Him, of walking with Him, and being face to face with Him. Yes, this is for us! The Holy Spirit's glory is found in us; therefore, we move and breathe and operate with Him always in us. From that perspective, we begin to look at our own image a little differently. We move from glory to glory when we realize that we already have His presence in us fully and yet we can always receive more and live in a place of overflow.

Seeing ourselves the way God sees us is crucial to becoming someone who stands on a firm foundation. If we let the world tell us who we are, that foundation will break. We could be successful, rich, funny, and good-looking, but if we don't know who we are, we will eventually break, because we will always feel empty deep down. Only God can tell us who we are. Only He can give us true happiness, true joy, and true fulfillment. That is what it looks like to build our lives on a firm foundation. One of the best things I did to discover my identity was to first read the Bible about the truth of who God is and who I am. But I went deeper. I asked God three questions that changed my life. Are you ready for them? Are you willing to go deeper with your relationship with God?

- What did you create me for?
- How much do you love me?
- What did you create me for to give me the most fulfillment in my life?

God is always good and God is always speaking. He wants more than anything to have a real, intimate relationship where He speaks to us. If we listen to what God says, we will never question our purpose or identity because that is our foundation. If we recognize the love He has for us, and the specific plans and purposes, we won't be shaken by what life throws at us because we've built our lives upon the truth of a promise spoken to us! *This* is the goodness of our God, of a loving father.

YOU'RE ON GOD'S PAYROLL

Tina:

So many people are turned off by religion, and let me tell you, so am I. I'm a Christian and when someone tries to shove "religion" in my face I get offensive and offended. Let's stop telling people how to live and just *show* them how to live.

I teach a lot of leadership classes, and I have T-shirts that say "Get Your Leadership On!" Last year I crossed out the word "Leadership" with a red X and replaced it with the word "Love." And it's true! You want to lead well? Then love well. That's what Jesus did. Right to the end. If you want to study the ultimate leader, study Jesus.

Love is a verb. We can't just say "I love you," we must demonstrate "I love you." The best way to get our love on is to be constantly renewed in our minds and to always have a fresh mental and spiritual attitude. Check out 2 Peter 1:5–7 (ESV):

> For this very reason, make every effort to supplement your faith with virtue, and virtue with knowledge, and knowledge with self-control, and self-control with steadfastness, and steadfastness with godliness, and godliness with brotherly affection, and brotherly affection with love.

Let that sink in:

- Faith
- Virtue
- Knowledge
- Self-control
- Steadfastness
- Godliness
- Brotherly affection
- Love

That's our job description. As a business owner I would love it if all of my staff (including me) excelled in all of these areas And think of this as a child of God: we work for God, so we're on His payroll!

Brianna:

"Blessed be the Lord, who daily loads us with benefits" (Psalm 68:19, NKJV).

"For His anger is but for a moment, His favor is for life" (Psalm 30:5, NKJV).

God has given us permission to be successful. His provision and His favor are meant for us. We have to stop looking at what's hard and start looking at the reward. Life is hard; we will do hard things and go through difficulties, but learning to trust God and persevere through all seasons will determine our reward. There is something about not giving up. Anyone who succeeds in life will tell you they are where they are today because they didn't give up.

Trusting God's Word and trusting His promises for us leads to a life of abundance. It takes risk to let go and trust God with our lives. Not just in one area, but in every area of life. There is provision for those who fully surrender their lives, hopes, and dreams to a God who loves us. There is abundance and favor for those who say yes to Jesus and say yes to the calling and purpose He has for us.

YOU ARE ARMED AND DANGEROUS

Tina:

> Put on the whole armor of God, that you may be able to stand against the schemes of the devil. For we do not wrestle against flesh and blood, but against the rulers, against the authorities, against the cosmic powers over this present darkness, against the spiritual forces of evil in the heavenly places. Therefore take up the whole armor of God, that you may be able to withstand in the evil day, and having done all, to stand firm.
> Ephesians 6:11–13 (ESV)

We are *armed and dangerous!*

Imagine you have a belt with ten holes in it. The belt stands for God's truth (His Word) and when you are tempted or in trouble, you tighten the belt a notch. When you worry, you tighten it a notch. When you lose your joy, you tighten it a notch. When you lose your peace, you tighten it a few more notches.

Decide now to stand firm, as the scripture says. Stand on God's Word. Don't just try on His Word; stand on it. You are armed and dangerous and you don't even know it. It's as if a man was attacking your child with a knife and ready to kill him, and you were just standing there. You forgot you have a gun in your pocket and you could shoot him before he does more harm. So it is with God's Word. You sit there depressed, stressed out, frustrated, or worse, but you have God's Word to combat it all. You are armed and dangerous.

Remember Hebrews 4:12 (NKJV):

> For the word of God is living and powerful, and sharper than any two-edged sword, piercing even to the division of soul and spirit, and of joints and marrow, and is a discerner of the thoughts and intents of the heart.

Give Satan the one-two punch—two quick blows to knock him out:

> **CALM DOWN:** "Peace I leave with you; my peace I give you. I do not give to you as the world gives. Do not let your hearts be troubled and do not be afraid" (John 14:27, NIV).

> **CHEER UP:** "I have told you these things, so that in me you may have peace. In this world you will have trouble. But take heart! I have overcome the world" (John 16:33, NIV).

Recently my husband and I had been on a long trip and we couldn't remember where we'd parked our car at the airport. We spent three hours searching the two possible parking lots for our car, and at the same time my iPhone stopped working—and we all know the dependence we have on our phones!

We kept our poise, got a hotel room, and decided to regroup in the morning. I literally applied the two-punch (out loud, in front of my husband—yes, I was giggling) and went to get a cup of coffee while he called the parking structure to report the car missing. Lo and behold, the guy working the desk told him they found our car. Now that's a quick one-two punch. Literally within ten minutes, God came through for us.

The fact is, you can release God's Word through prayer, confessing His Word out loud, and taking God-inspired action!

Brianna:

The enemy wants nothing more than to get you to believe the lie that you aren't powerful. It started in the Garden of Eden, when he convinced Adam and Eve that they didn't need God. What was the result? Shame. Adam and Eve once walked with God, as friends of God, but once they believed the devil, they no longer walked hand-in-hand with God. Instead, they hid from Him, filled with shame and fear.

If the devil can get you to go through life without discovering your God-given identity and purpose, you will feel powerless. So how do you destroy a lie? You feed it truth.

God created you for such a time as this! He has placed you and planted you to be a voice, to stand in your identity, and be a powerful representation of Him on the earth. God's love, power, and joy rest on you, and Jesus paid the ultimate price for you to come into the fullness of who He is in you.

1 John 4:17 (AMP) says, "As He is, so are we in this world."

You have authority. God has given you authority to:

1. Stand confident in who you are
2. Help other people discover their identity
3. Destroy the lies of the devil

> That day when evening came, He said to His disciples, "Let us go over to the other side." Leaving the crowd behind, they took Him along, just as He was, in the boat. There were also other boats with Him. A furious squall came up, and the waves broke over the boat, so that it was nearly swamped. Jesus was in the stern,

> sleeping on a cushion. The disciples woke Him and said to Him, "Teacher, don't you care if we drown?" He got up, rebuked the wind and said to the waves, "Quiet! Be still!" Then the wind died down and it was completely calm. He said to His disciples, "Why are you so afraid? Do you still have no faith?" They were terrified and asked each other, "Who is this? Even the wind and the waves obey Him!"
>
> Mark 4:35–41

Bill Johnson, senior pastor of Bethel Church and one of my favorite pastors, says, "You have authority over any storm you can sleep in." If you want to grow in authority, you have to be willing to open your mouth. Jesus rebuked the waves and released peace. Jesus is filled with peace: He doesn't know anything else, it is His internal reality that became external. What does that mean for us? If we want to have authority over storms in our lives, it starts with our hearts. It starts with believing that "As He is, so am I." When our internal reality becomes external, we walk through life ready and able to conquer and rebuke every storm. The renewed mind lives in constant awareness of every internal victory in Christ.

STEP 4 EXERCISE: **SCRIPTURES FOR UNCOMMON DISCIPLINE**

The scriptures talk about uncommon discipline. As you reflect on these verses, write a note below each one about how it applies to you.

- **Hebrews 12:11**: "No discipline seems pleasant at the time, but painful. Later on, however, it produces a harvest of righteousness and peace for those who have been trained by it."

- **1 Timothy 4:7 (AMP)**: "But have nothing to do with irreverent folklore and silly myths. On the other hand, discipline yourself for the purpose of godliness [keeping yourself spiritually fit]."

- **1 Corinthians 9:24–25 (AMP)**: "Do you not know that in a race all the runners run [their very best to win] but only one receives the prize? Run [your race] in such a way that you may seize the prize and make it yours! Now every athlete who [goes into training and] competes in the games is disciplined and exercises self-control in all things. They do it to win a crown that withers, but we [do it to receive] an imperishable [crown that cannot wither]."

- **2 Timothy 1:7**: "For the Spirit God gave us does not make us timid, but gives us power, love and self-discipline."

- **1 Corinthians 9:27 (AMP)**: "But [like a boxer] I strictly discipline my body and make it my slave, so that, after I have preached [the gospel] to others, I myself will not somehow be disqualified [as unfit for service]."

What other verses could you add to this list?

THE POWER OF LEGACY

Brianna:

Living an uncommon life comes down to living a life of surrender and learning to posture our hearts as a lover of Jesus. As we discover Him, we discover ourselves.

Being unsure of our future or wondering what our purpose is can be stressful. In a generation where anxiety is the norm, we have to fight to stay in God's presence. We have to fight to stay in rest and stay in peace. When we fight for that place, we find that God is all we need.

Being secure in our identity as a child of God always starts with surrender and getting into His presence. He will work out every detail of our lives; we have to trust Him. it might not always be easy, but it's worth it.

- Matthew 11:28–30 (TPT) says, "Are you weary, carrying a heavy burden? Then come to me. I will refresh your life, for I am your oasis. Simply join your life with mine. Learn my ways and you'll discover that I'm gentle, humble, easy to please. You will find refreshment and rest in me. For all that I require of you will be pleasant and easy to bear."
- Romans 11:29 says, "For God's gifts and His call are irrevocable." They cannot be taken away from you.

- Isaiah 55:11 says, "So is my word that goes out from my mouth: It will not return to me empty, but will accomplish what I desire and achieve the purpose for which I sent it."

Don't limit what God can do through the lens of your life but rather through the lens of eternity and your legacy. No matter what your past is, how you grew up, the thoughts and behaviors you've had before, today is a new day. Never confuse your current situation, for God's portion He has already given you. It's time to step into your destiny. It's time to start believing what God has said about you.

God wants to use your life to bring about a legacy only He could design for you and your family. He created you on purpose, and for such a time as this. God has placed gifts and callings on you, not just for yourself, but to impact generations. This is what legacy is all about: making an impact. You are called, you have a voice, and you are affecting and influencing every generation to follow.

Tina:

I want to speak to parents right now because I truly believe that God gave us the children that we have to teach us and perfect us. I believe our children are better versions of us. Instead of trying to mold them to be like us, we need to empower and equip them to be like Jesus. How we respond will affect generations to come.

THE POWER OF LEGACY

Remember this: If you are a child of God, and you believe in the promises He speaks over you in His Word, then *you are uncommon*. Uncommon people have uncommon plans, uncommon friends, uncommon thoughts, and uncommon discipline.

You are a miracle in motion! As my friend and pastor Tim Storey says, you are a world shaker, a history maker. Now go out there and live an *uncommon* life. Let your light shine.

There is power in your legacy, and God has created you to have a champion spirit!

ACKNOWLEDGMENTS

This book was inspired by a pastor, speaker, world shaker, and friend of ours, Tim Storey. The moment I heard him speak about being uncommon, I knew I needed to tell the world. Tim has written several books, offers many incredible courses (including "Making Your Dreams a Reality"), and he pastors a wonderful church in Placentia, California. He's one of the greatest mentors in my life and he has truly taught me how to be a difference right where I am in business and how to be in marketplace ministry.

– Tina Black

ADDITIONAL RESOURCES

Tina Black: www.TinaBlack.net
Tina Black Podcast: The BE Series – Untold Stories of Leadership Transformation
Tim Storey: www.timstorey.com
Joyce Meyer: www.joycemeyer.org
John C. Maxwell monthly messages: www.johnmaxwellacademy.com
Bright Pink: www.brightpink.org

ABOUT THE AUTHORS

Tina Black owns four Paul Mitchell Schools, co-owns three salons (Paul Mitchell The Salon, The Salon Rochester, and The Salon Naples), has written four books, and is a popular speaker, coach, Mastermind leader, and host of the popular *Be Series* podcast. As an executive director with the John Maxwell Team and a certified trainer and coach, she has conducted nationwide values-based transformational leadership initiatives with Maxwell at the invitation of governments in Guatemala and Costa Rica. After a long career as a dental hygienist, Tina purchased and graduated from her own cosmetology school, which quickly became one of the ten original Paul Mitchell Schools. She has held many roles in her schools; she co-created the student-run Be Nice Teams now offered in every Paul Mitchell School; and she worked closely with Dr. Susan Swearer, professor of School Psychology for the University of Nebraska–Lincoln, to write a self-empowerment and anti-bullying curriculum for all Paul Mitchell Schools. Tina's schools have been recognized with facilities, leadership, culture, and other awards within the network, and they regularly rank among the top ten in the annual FUNraising campaign, which has raised millions of dollars for charity since 2004.

Tina has spent countless hours becoming the leader, mentor, keynote speaker, and author she is today. She plans to open more schools and salons, and to mentor and motivate everyone she meets. She firmly believes in "people before profit" and she often says, "I'm in the business of changing lives."

Brianna Black-Petros is the education and training director and co-owner of three Paul Mitchell The Salon locations. As the daughter of successful Paul Mitchell School owners, she grew up in the industry. She attended cosmetology school while she was still in high school and graduated after learning from and being mentored by beauty industry legends Kelly Cardenas and Vivienne Mackinder. Brianna completed the instructor course and joined the first management team at Paul Mitchell The School Fort Myers (Florida). Committed to helping girls who have been rescued from sex trafficking, Brianna raised more than $100,000 for an orphanage and cosmetology training center in Nepal to teach young girls victimized by sex-trafficking the skills to prepare them for careers in cosmetology. She also opened a safe-home cosmetology school and served as an international cosmetology educator for Angel House Ministries in Nepal. Since 2014, she has been a John Maxwell Team makeup artist and coach.

Brianna has been featured in *O Magazine* and worked with celebrity hairstylist Ken Paves on the *Biggest Loser* TV series. She works closely with local photographers, shooting special occasions and teen editorial projects. She is a top referral for weddings in Michigan and Florida, specializing in long-hair design, cutting, color, and airbrush makeup. Brianna loves using her creativity to help people fall in love with their hair.

Most important, she is a wife and mother of a one-year-old son, and expecting her second child in August 2020.

CPSIA information can be obtained
at www.ICGtesting.com
Printed in the USA
FSHW021455271020

9 781647 730482